THE ULTIMATE ANIMAL LIBRARY

Tiger Sharks

by Janie Scheffer

BLASTOFF! READERS 2

BELLWETHER MEDIA • MINNEAPOLIS, MN

Blastoff! Readers are carefully developed by literacy experts to build reading stamina and move students toward fluency by combining standards-based content with developmentally appropriate text.

Level 1 provides the most support through repetition of high-frequency words, light text, predictable sentence patterns, and strong visual support.

Level 2 offers early readers a bit more challenge through varied sentences, increased text load, and text-supportive special features.

Level 3 advances early-fluent readers toward fluency through increased text load, less reliance on photos, advancing concepts, longer sentences, and more complex special features.

★ **Blastoff! Universe**

Reading Level

Grade
K

Grades
1–3

Grade
4

This edition first published in 2026 by Bellwether Media, Inc.

No part of this publication may be reproduced in whole or in part without written permission of the publisher. For information regarding permission, write to Bellwether Media, Inc., Attention: Permissions Department, 3500 American Blvd W, Suite 150, Bloomington, MN 55431.

Library of Congress Cataloging-in-Publication Data

LC record for Tiger Sharks available at: https://lccn.loc.gov/2025003948

Text copyright © 2026 by Bellwether Media, Inc. BLASTOFF! READERS and associated logos are trademarks and/or registered trademarks of Bellwether Media, Inc. Bellwether Media is a division of FlutterBee Education Group.

Editor: Elizabeth Neuenfeldt Series Designer: Veah Demmin

Printed in the United States of America, North Mankato, MN.

Table of Contents

What Are Tiger Sharks?

Tiger sharks are among the largest sharks in the world. These fish are known to eat anything! They are mostly found in **tropical** ocean waters.

Tiger Shark Report
Range
N
W
E
S
range =
Status in the Wild
near threatened
Habitat
oceans

Tiger sharks are named for the stripes on their backs. These stripes fade as they get older.

Their bellies are white.
Their skin colors help them
hide in the water.

Tiger sharks have strong, **slender** bodies.

Tiger sharks have wide heads. They have big eyes and short **snouts**.

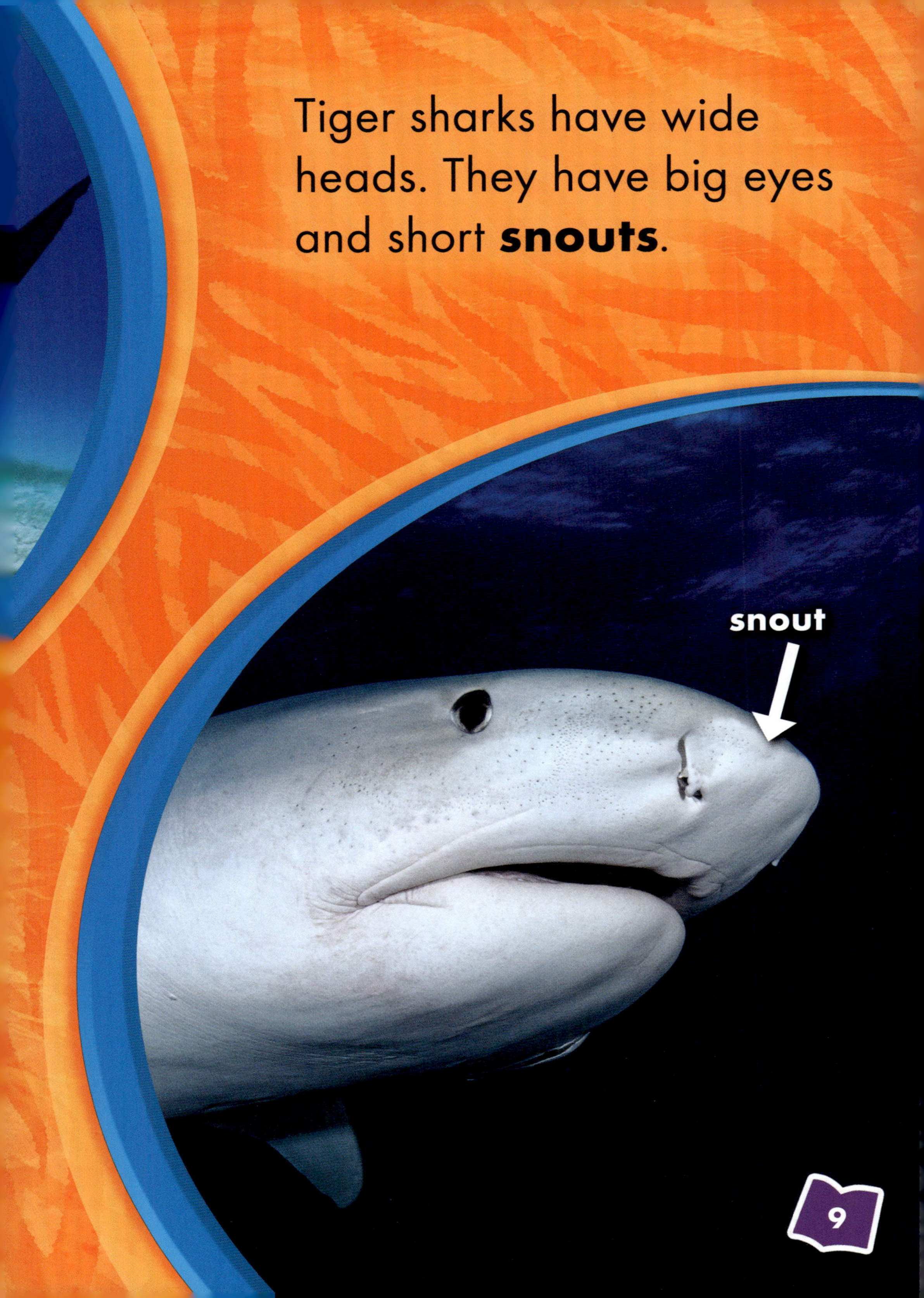

Tiger sharks have rows of **jagged** teeth. Their teeth help them hold and tear **prey**.

They also have very powerful jaws. They can crush sea turtle shells!

Spot a Tiger Shark
stripes on back
short snout
slender body

Hungry Hunters!

Tiger sharks usually live alone. They are mostly found near **coasts**.

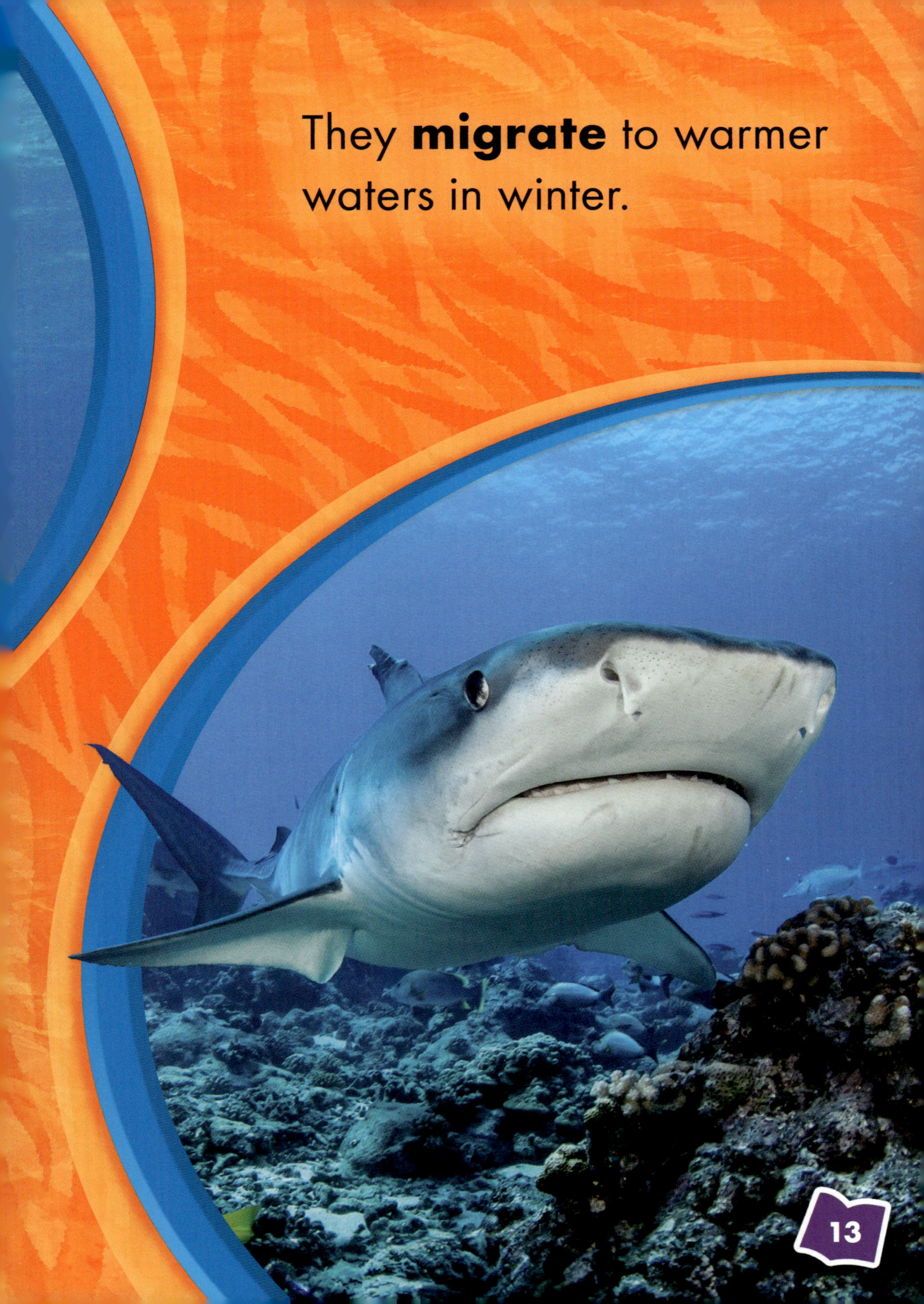

They **migrate** to warmer waters in winter.

Tiger sharks are **nocturnal** and hunt at night. They can easily see and smell prey.

They follow their prey slowly.
Then they quickly attack!

Tiger sharks are **carnivores**. They eat stingrays, seals, and seabirds. They also eat sea turtles.

They are sometimes hunted by orcas.

Growing Up

Tiger sharks **mate** every three years. Mothers give birth to **pups**.

A **litter** can have as many as 82 pups!

pup

Pups live on their own right away. They reach adulthood by seven years old.

These hungry hunters can live up to 50 years!

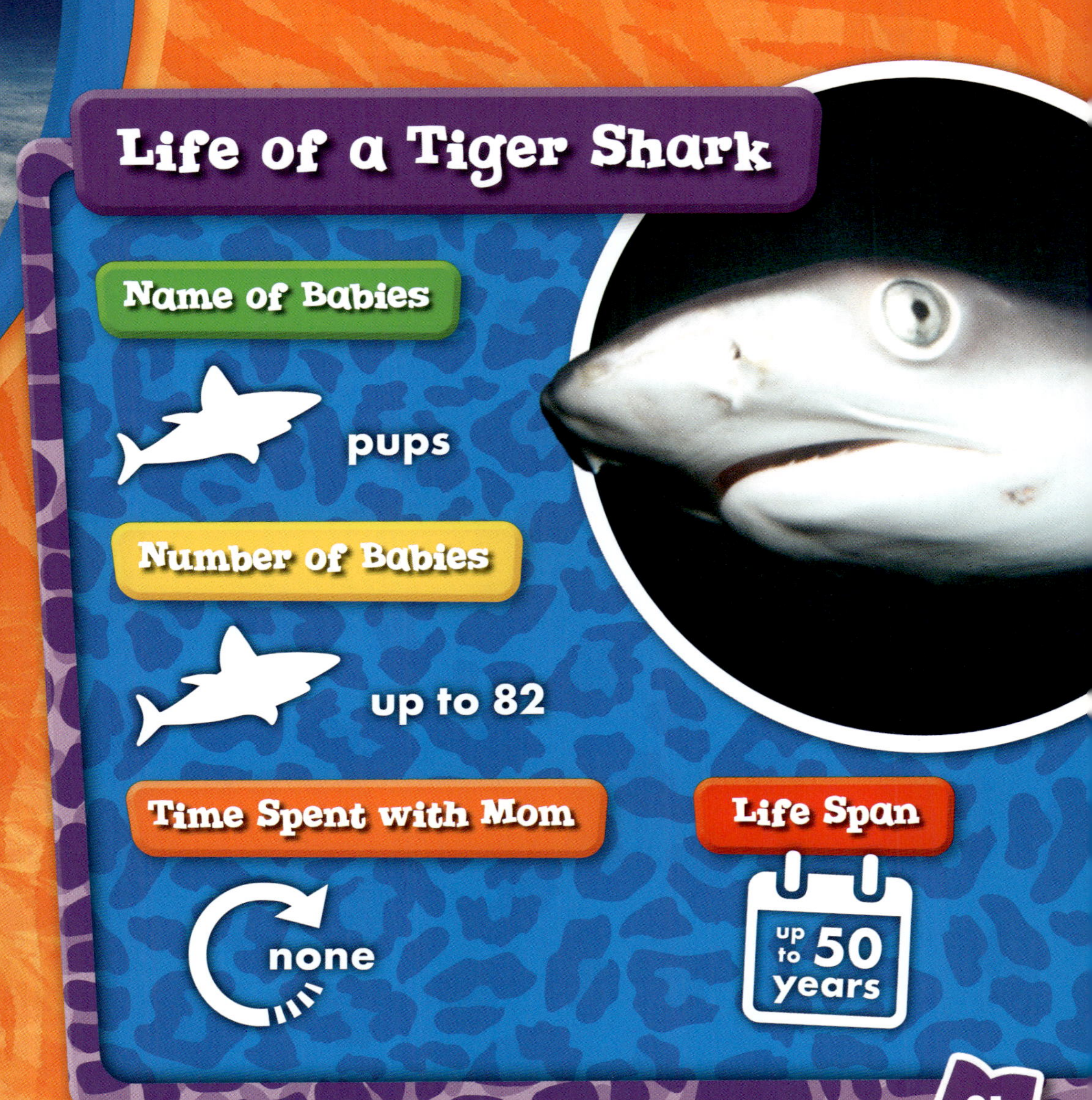

Glossary

carnivores—animals that only eat meat

coasts—lands near water

jagged—having points that are sharp or uneven

litter—a group of baby animals born at one time

mate—to join together to make young

migrate—to travel from one place to another, often with the seasons

nocturnal—active at night

prey—animals that are hunted by other animals for food

pups—baby tiger sharks

slender—thin

snouts—the noses and mouths of some animals

tropical—related to places that are hot and humid

To Learn More

AT THE LIBRARY

Andrews, E. C. *Tiger Shark Files.* Minneapolis, Minn.: Bearport Publishing Company, 2025.

Humphrey, Natalie. *Tiger Shark vs. Praying Mantis.* New York, N.Y.: Gareth Stevens Publishing, 2023.

Storm, Marysa. *Tiger Sharks.* Mankato, Minn.: Black Rabbit Books, 2024.

ON THE WEB

FACTSURFER

Factsurfer.com gives you a safe, fun way to find more information.

1. Go to www.factsurfer.com.
2. Enter "tiger sharks" into the search box and click .

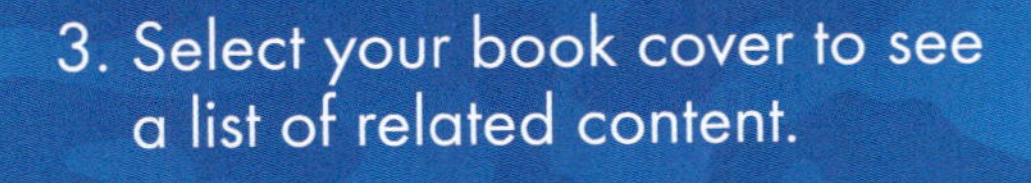

3. Select your book cover to see a list of related content.

Index

The images in this book are reproduced through the courtesy of: frantisekhojdysz, cover (tiger shark); Damsea, cover background, interior background; frantisek hojdysz, pp. 3, 10-11, 11, 23; yoshinori, p. 4; Aaron, p. 6; hakbak, p. 7; wildestanimal, pp. 8, 17 (orcas); Martin, p. 9; Matt9122, p. 10; Carlos, p. 12; Tropicalens, p. 13; Daniel Lamborn, pp. 14, 18; izenkai, p. 15; lego 19861111, pp. 16-17; steff enw, p. 17 (seabirds); VisionDive, p. 17 (tiger shark); dam, p. 17 (stingrays); jdawg316, p. 17 (seals); ArteSub/ Alamy, pp. 18-19, 21; MDay Photography, p. 20.